FISHING DIRTY TRICKS

By Glen-Bob Smith and Ray Villwock
Illustrations by Barrie Maguire

Dedication from Glen-Bob Smith: To Mom, who always reeled me in when I got out of line.
Dedication from Ray Villwock: To Alexis, who never stoops to dirty tricks.

www.andrewsmcmeel.com

ISBN: 0-8362-4953-4

Fishing Dirty Tricks is produced by becker&mayer!, Ltd.

Book illustrations by Barrie Maguire
Art direction by Simon Sung
Production and layout by Isiah T. Armstead
Edited by Jennifer Worick

FISHING DIRTY TRICKS
50 Ways to Lie and Cheat Your Way to a Really Big Fish

By Bob Smith and Ray Villwock
Illustrations by Barrie Maguire

**Andrews McMeel
Publishing**

Kansas City

For some, fishing is a way to kick back and relax . . . to get close to nature . . . or to bring home some tasty meals and have fun at the same time. For others, it's a way to stack up dead fish like cordwood . . . to show off and humiliate those less fortunate in their catch . . . to prove once and for all who's the best. If you're one of these folks—this book is for you!

Whether you're fishing in a professional tournament for big bucks, just out with your neighbor, or any variation in between, you can use these dirty tricks to ensure that you come home on top.

Not only are the following tips guaranteed to make you a winner, they can be used anytime, anyplace—on anyone.

Bigger Is Better

Sneaky Ways to Improve Your Catch

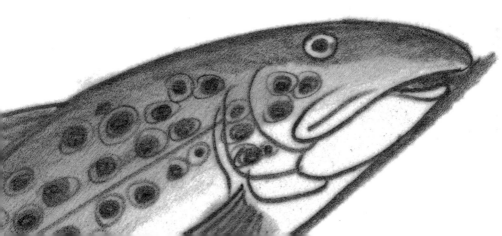

The Phony Tape Measure

There's no easier way to stomp your fellow angler into the ground—and turn him red with rage—than to use the special tape measure that's included with this book. The sneaky tape lets you build a big lead over anyone. No need to toss back those 6-inchers that are under the legal limit—they measure a respectable 12 inches on your special ruler! Your rival will watch in disbelief as you keep fish after fish he thought was below the limit. And if he dares to challenge you, simply hold up the fish and ruler side by side and say with an air of concern, "Maybe you need to get your eyes checked."

The Weight–and–See Approach

This trick takes balls—tiny lead balls, that is. Secretly drop lead pellets down the gullet of your fish before having it weighed. You can easily add 4, 5, even 10 ounces to your catch's weight. Be sure to keep the weight gain believable, though—you don't want to dump a pound of lead down the throat of a 10-inch bass.

Note: NEVER turn the fish upside down.

The Photo Extender

Here's another easy one: No matter how big or how small your fish, just hold it out in front of you as far as you can while a photo of your catch is being snapped. The camera will do the rest—dramatically increasing the apparent size of your prize.

Photo Extender 2

A more sophisticated version of the Photo Extender. Simply have the back end of a fish silk-screened onto the lower half of a T-shirt. Then, when you catch one of those small fish, hold it against the T-shirt with the head of the fish held close to the photo. The back half will blend into the shirt photo—and your fish will suddenly "grow" 6 to 12 inches (depending on the size of your gut).

A Stretch in Time

Perfect for that tournament when you've forgotten your phony tape measure, or someone has actually challenged your measurement, is the old "shoe-stretcher" trick. You have to obtain a professional stretcher, which is a wooden shoe-like contraption with a turning screw on the end. Keep it handy in your tackle box, and when you hook a bass or trout that's just below keeper size, you shove the stretcher down its mouth—and turn, turn, turn. You'll be amazed how quickly you can make that fish legal. This works especially well for sole.

Fish Out of Water

There's no better way to build a reputation as the king fisherman on the block than to go off by yourself and constantly return home with a stringer of beauties. You never fail, much to the annoyance of other anglers in your neighborhood, who constantly have their spouses throwing your success up to their faces. Now, you could actually go and catch the fish—but then you wouldn't need this book. The tricky way is to simply locate a few fish markets in nearby towns that are open on weekends and make sure they have your "catch" put aside. You then pull up, transfer those babies from the fish market's cooler to your own ice chest, and the rest of the day is yours to do whatever you want. One warning: Never, never, NEVER say where you caught them. If you do, sooner or later your jealous neighbors will insist on accompanying you to see you in action. And if you fail . . . well, a lynch mob is not a pretty sight.

Get a Long, Little Fishy

If your reputation as an angler is hanging by a thread, boost it fast by keeping a small sewing kit in your tackle box. When you catch two relatively small fish, cut the head off one and the tail off the other— then sew the two bodies together. Get yourself snapped holding up the spliced fish. Nobody will notice the stitches in your finny patient unless you show the photo to a sharp-eyed surgeon (or to Dr. Frankenstein). Don't get fancy; cross-stitching subliminal messages is too time-consuming.

Minnow to Monster

You're headed back to the dock or weigh-in area with little to show for the hard day you've put in, and you just know your most hated rival will be there with a big stringer of fat beauties and a gloating smile on his ugly face. All you've got are a few anorexic-looking bodies that barely deserve to be called fish. Don't despair. Hardware stores sell a sturdy balloon-like device that attaches to garden hoses to unclog drains. Keep a few of these on hand for emergencies like this. Insert one balloon inside each of those skinny minnies, and blow that sucker up with water. Those sturdy balloons will instantly stretch them into fatter-looking fish, and will add weight as well. Just be ready for some "Gee, those fish look awfully potbellied" remarks. If it's the spawning season you've got a ready explanation; if not, point out that fish don't have access to fitness videos.

Unbalancing Acts

Acts

Freaking Out Your Foes

The Cast Blast

Here's an easy way to annoy your rival: Whenever he makes a cast, you immediately cast to the same spot. Mutter "Sorry" each time—but keep doing it for the first dozen or so casts. Make sure you're using an oversize bait too, so it makes a nice big "splat" when it hits the water. Although this won't help you catch more fish, it's guaranteed to drive the other guy crazy. Even when you start throwing your bait to spots of your own, he'll continue to keep a wary eye on you instead of paying full attention to what he's doing. By day's end, you'll have buried him.

Getting an Eyeful

Nothing wrecks your rival's concentration like a few wild backcasts from you. The key is placing your lure extremely close to his face as you whip it back to cast. A lure full of treble hooks missing his eye by a sixteenth of an inch is the perfect backcast. When you're a graduate trickster, you can accomplish this without ever turning your head to look back at all— and that's guaranteed to shatter his nerves. If his nerves don't go first, he'll soon be throwing his own bait into trees, rocks, and weeds—and you win again.

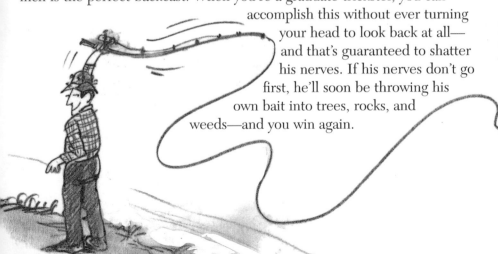

Iced Out

Nothing gives the tricky fisherman more pleasure than a successful sneak attack on a fellow angler's waders. Hearing icy water sloshing around inside his boots or watching him turn blue from the cold—or, best of all, listening to his teeth chatter when he tries to speak—will warm any trickster's heart. An ice pick is the ticket. You don't want to use a fillet knife because it leaves an easily spotted, incriminating gash—and you'll be the No.1 suspect if you're carrying a matching blade. When your foe isn't looking, a quick poke in the boot area of the wader ensures some icy toes. Your opposition will be blue in more ways than one.

Of course, it's best to do this when he isn't wearing the wader. Otherwise it becomes assault with a deadly weapon instead of just a dirty fishing trick.

Setting the Record Straight

If you aren't included in the fishing record books, include yourself. Superimpose your name over a champion's name in a world record book. Then photocopy the page and enlarge it on the copy machine. Stick it in a flashy frame and show it off to intimidate all your fishing pals.

Note: This trick works best if you're new in town.

Looking Sharp

Arrive with two suspicious-looking poles among your fishing rods. The end of one pole has a sleeve fitting, so it's clear the two fit together to form a 10-foot pole. Next, allow your opponents to see that you've also brought along a huge five-pronged spearhead with a sleeve that obviously fits the pole.

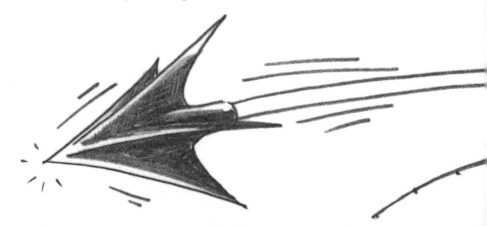

When someone protests, you shrug and say, "Spear? What spear? This is a lure retriever" or "Aw, it's just protection in case a bear comes around" (a good response when you're fishing in, say, a lake in the middle of Cleveland). This is a ploy intended to rattle the competition only. Don't get carried away and actually use the spear; those tell-tale holes are mighty incriminating.

Looking Sharper

What's more pathetic than a trout stream swarming with fish where it's strictly catch-and-release and fly-fishing only? To address this intolerable situation: Show up in a T-shirt, dirty torn jeans, carrying a 6-pack of Bud and a patched-up rod. As your fellow fly-fishers look at you with disdain, you casually call out, "How's the fishing? I really *killed* them here last week." Draped across your back is a deadly looking high–tech CROSSBOW!

Confronted with a serial fish murderer, the purists will run away in horror, leaving behind their obscenely expensive, obnoxious bamboo poles. That night you can fry your tasty catch on a nice bamboo-fueled campfire.

By Hook or Crook

Sabotage

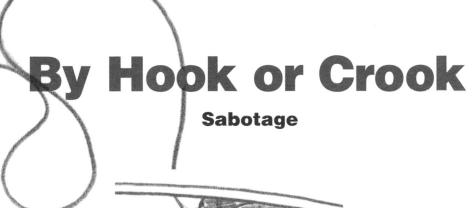

Hook, Line . . . and Sinker

Ah, there's nothing like the sight of a fishing boat—especially when it's sinking and belongs to someone you're out to beat. Sure, every fisherman knows he's supposed to check the transom drain plug on his boat before he backs the boat down the ramp, but almost every one of us has forgotten at least once. So your foe will never suspect you, if you do this right. The key is timing. You've carefully watched your victim check out his boat, including the plug. Now he's back by the car, relaxed and waiting his turn to launch his boat. That's when you stealthily approach, drop something to the ground behind his boat, bend down to retrieve it—and give a quick turn and yank to his plug. Then you just stand back and watch, ready with a sympathetic word, while his boat slowly sinks lower and lower.

Down to the Sea in Ships

If you're lucky enough to be involved in a contest in which everyone's boats are in the water overnight and you're all scheduled to start out around the same time in the morning, this trick is especially effective. Sneak out in the middle of the night and loosen the transom plug so it's just barely in there. That way the boats won't sink while at the dock. (It would look a trifle suspicious if everyone's boat but yours was underwater in the morning.) But when your rivals kick their boats

up to roar off to their favorite fishing spots, sooner or later that loose plug will pull out—and you'll be a sure winner. Best you don't do this on a really deep lake, or in an ocean tournament, unless you really, really, really dislike the other contestants—and you have a very good lawyer.

Flying Off the Handle

This is an especially satisfying way to humiliate your rival—by striking at the very heart of his sport, his handling of a rod and reel. First, you secretly loosen the side plate screws on his reel. Sooner or later, as he casts, the reel will misfire. If you're really lucky, the whole thing will come flying apart and spook the fish in his hole for hours.

You offer condolences—and the use of one of your own outfits. When he casts it, the top half of the two-piece rod will fly off—because you've cleverly loosened that beforehand, too. Your shaken opponent won't manage a decent cast the rest of the day.

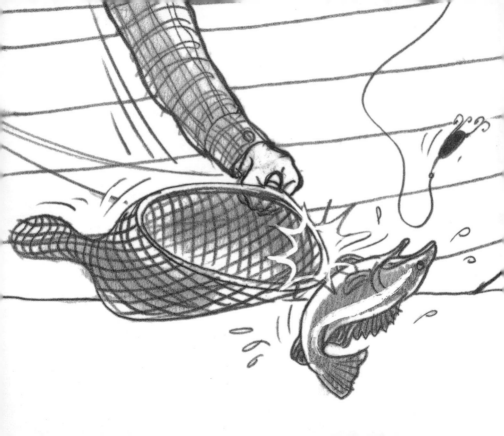

Letting Him Off the Hook

As you lean over to net your rival's fish, you clumsily miss and utter a loud "Oops!" When he gets the fish close again, you lean over—and miss again, calling for an even louder "Oops!" The third time is the charm. On this try you "accidentally" hit the fish close to its mouth, which should dislodge the hook. If the hook doesn't pop right out, whack the fish with the net again, muttering something about "the damn fish tried to bite me." Not only will your rival lose a fish—he'll be a bundle of jangled nerves the next time he hooks one, wondering how the heck he's going to get it in the boat.

DIRTY TRICK #19

The Clean and Jerk

You have to be fast to pull off this trick, but it CAN be done. Wait until your fishing partner backcasts and his lure is behind him—then quickly hook it into something solid, such as the seat of the boat. As your unsuspecting opponent whips his rod forward, his body will come to a grinding halt—almost certainly pulling at least one major muscle and putting him out of action (and maybe into traction).

The Net–Loss Ploy

Facing a really tough foe? Stealthily move the landing net directly behind him. Within minutes, he'll hook the net with his backcast and either flip it out of the boat or hit himself in the back with it. He'll be so mortified (thanks mainly to your loud, continual guffaw) that he won't be the same for hours.

Thinking Deep

Some dirty tricks are just . . . well . . . dirty. But this one is for the deep thinker. In today's high-tech fishing world, a depth finder is a vital piece of equipment. Modern depth finders are not only very sensitive and pick up fish at very shallow levels, they even display them as little fishlike figures on the screen. That's where you come in. You attach some fishlike figures made of wood to 5–10 feet of fishing line. Then tie the fishing line to your rival's transducer, which is the "eye" of the depth finder, located underwater on the transom. When he gets to the fishing ground, he'll turn on his depth finder—and "wow," instant fish. No matter where he goes, he'll be looking at schools on his screen—and he'll be tearing his hair out all day long trying to catch those elusive "fish." You'll be laughing all the way to the trophy weigh-in as you watch him constantly fishing where there are only timber denizens of the deep.

The Splashdown

At strategic moments, such as when your opponent is about to set the hook on a fish or has one playing with his bait, you suddenly make a HUGE splash. You can "accidentally" drop a paddle in the water, or knock a bucket overboard—or, in a pinch, pretend to slip and slap the water with your hand. Warning: If you do this too often, the next splash you hear could be your partner throwing you overboard.

The Slam Dunk

A personal favorite. It's every bit as satisfying as stuffing a basketball through the hoop, and it's a lot easier. Just about everybody has experienced the sickening sensation of realizing you've just slammed the car door on one of your fishing rods, so you've already got experience at this. As you load your rival's rods in the car prior to a fishing outing, you make sure they "accidentally" slip down so that the tips are placed in the path of the closing door. Then you give the door your best Arnold Schwarzenegger and really slam it home. You'll hear two sounds. The first will be the snap, crackle, pop of his rods. The second sound will be his anguished yelp. Then you deliver a snide "Sorrrry."

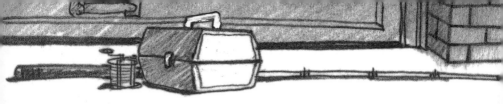

The Mini–Dunk

If snapping your foe's rod tips is too violent for you,
simply leave his tackle box and one or more of his best
rod-and-reel outfits behind during loading. Mention your
Marine Corps training (even if you don't have any) as you
volunteer to stow all the gear in the back. "I'm good at
making things shipshape—I'll get everything in with
room to spare," you assure him. Naturally, you leave
something strategic behind. Smoke will come out of
his ears when he discovers at river's edge that he
doesn't have the vital equipment you've "forgotten."
That's when you'll be glad you made that Marine
Corps remark—it'll keep him from doing more
than fuming.

The Splash Dunk

Yet another variation of the Slam Dunk. This time you allow your opponent to arrive with all his gear intact. If he starts getting lucky look for the moment to strike. That moment comes when your rival has left his tackle box open and turns his head, or when he has precariously balanced his rod and reel on the edge of the boat. Then you casually dump the tackle box over, preferably in the water. Or you knock the rod overboard. Of course, you quickly utter that by-now familiar "Oops!"

Brake Dance

You say your obnoxious neighbor likes to brag about how he catches more fish than you? Here's a perfect way to put him in his place. Challenge him to meet you at a certain lake where you'll go boat-to-boat with him. But just before dawn, you sneak over and poke out his boat trailer brake lights. So far, pretty tame, huh? Now, here's where that special dirty-trickster touch comes in: Not only do you call the highway patrol and tell them a guy is trailering a boat without brake lights down the road to Lake So and-So, but you say you almost rear-ended the guy. And when you warned him his brake lights were out, he told you to get lost. Here's the best part: You tell the dispatcher that when you yelled he'd better watch out or the cops would get him, he yelled back: "Screw those highway patrol morons. They couldn't find ice at the North Pole. They'll never stop me." Depending on where you live, Mr. Neighbor could end up with a costly ticket AND a broken nose.

Better Loch Ness Time

Make no mistake about it: Lots of fishermen believe the depths are inhabited by strange creatures. How else to explain so many sightings of the Loch Ness Monster and other legendary beasts by anglers? To take advantage of this belief, you'll need to enlist a co-conspirator. Secretly build a Loch Ness–type monster by attaching half-tires to a submersible platform, then add a menacing-looking head with fangs. Paint the "creature" a sickly green. The final result should resemble a giant snake-like animal undulating through the water.

Hide the "monster" in a cove 50 yards up the river from where you and your fellow fishermen will be casting. Attach heavy fishing line to the platform, and station your friend out of sight on the opposite bank with the line in his hand. As everyone is fishing, yell: "LOOK!"—

and
that's the signal for your
pal to slowly tow the monster across
the river. Your opponents will freak out and
probably run home –leaving you all alone to enjoy
a nice day's fishing.

Bad Break

Use a saw to cut almost cleanly through the underside of the handle of the landing net you're taking to a big tournament. When your opponent reels in his biggest catch, volunteer to net it. Watch with hidden glee as the handle snaps, dumping his fish back in the water. While he sobs, you angrily mutter something about cheap foreign metal.

Note: If YOU hook the first big fish and he offers to net it for you, make sure he uses his own net!

A Bird's Nest in the Hand

There's nothing like the Mother of All Backlashes to wreck your opponent's day—and keep a smirk gracing the face of the tricky fisherman. If your rival is using a bait-casting reel, wait until his back is turned and loosen the side tension-adjustment knob on the reel. His next cast will cause such a horrible backlash that he'll tear out what little hair he has left. More important, either he's out of the game for many valuable minutes or he has to switch to a less-favored outfit. Either way, you win again.

Just for the Halibut

Halibut

A Potpourri of Far–Out Tricks

License to Grill

The keen-eyed dirty trickster is certain to note where his rival carries his fishing license. If it's in his tackle box, the guy is easy prey. And even if he wears his license on his fishing vest, no problem: Just give him a big old friendly hug to start off the day—and slip his proof-of-purchase into your hand. Drop it into the water or in the campfire without his knowledge. Then wait for the next check by the park ranger or game warden. You'll love watching your rival squirm as he tries to convince the warden that he really did have a fishing license. And you'll bury him the rest of the day as he fumes over his expensive citation instead of concentrating on catching fish.

If you're really good, you can increase the odds that a ranger will check his license. Just print out a sign in large letters with adhesive on the back and stick it on your rival's car bumper, or on the side of his boat, or maybe on the back of his tackle box. What should it say? "Game Wardens Suck" will work just fine.

The Turning Worm

Today you can buy very lifelike plastic worms that can be used in a master trickster's ploy. After you and your fellow suckers . . . er, fishermen . . . reach a "No Live Bait, Fly-Fishing Only" stream, casually drape a realistic-looking plastic worm on the end of your fly. Your horrified opponents will shout "Foul!" As you make your way downstream, you explain that it's only a special Russian "worm fly" you ordered from overseas. They'll seethe with suspicion, certain to fling their own first backcast into a tree as they cast ugly looks in your direction. But here's the master touch: You actually have real worms concealed in your jacket. And after your big display with the plastic worms ("See, they're plastic; they don't move"), you stealthily make the switch—and start pulling in hungry trout one after the other.

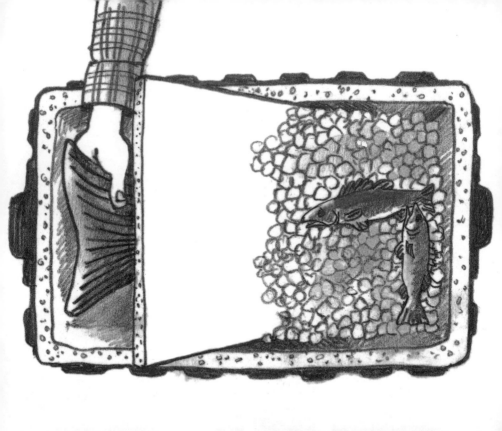

Playing It Close to the Chest

It's hard to get lower than this, but a cheater's gotta do what a cheater's gotta do. First buy a large styrofoam ice chest and a sheet of styrofoam from a supply house. Carefully craft a false bottom for the ice chest from the styrofoam sheet. Next, buy a big, beautiful fish from the local market the night before and conceal it in the false bottom. Now you literally have an ace in the hole. If all your other dirty tricks fail to work, you can always pull out the winner and shout "Voilà!" (Pronounce it "walleye.")

"Fishin': Impossible"

Ever wanted to be a master spy, a suave and cunning devil who can sneak into any high-security installation? Your mission, should you decide to accept it, is to launch a raid on a fish hatchery—where, as everyone knows, fishing is VERBOTEN. To do it right, plan your invasion like a military campaign. Don camouflage clothing—it helps you get into the spirit—and stake out the closest trout hatchery. If you can obtain night-vision goggles, get 'em and use 'em. Wait for the ideal time to penetrate the target's tight security, then GO FOR IT! Net the biggest trout you can find—don't worry, they can't scream and alert guards—then slip away with your Catch of the Night. (CAUTION: Anglers who've conducted these raids sometimes get carried away and find themselves lobbing grenades into the stream . . . Get a grip!)

Note: As usual, if you fail, the authors will disavow any knowledge of your mission.

Holy Mackerel

If you're spending a weekend fishing at a remote lake or river and find it teeming with finny critters, tell your fellow anglers you've heard tales that old Spanish missionaries blessed the most common species of fish there. According to legend, you say, anyone who kills that type of fish is doomed to a horrible death. Recount chilling stories of fishermen who died in gruesome ways.

Later you catch one of those fish—and attached to its lip is a tiny silver cross! Feigning horror, you throw it back in the water and run screaming from the site. Your competitors will never suspect that you secretly caught that fish earlier and attached the cross. If they're superstitious, they'll believe there really is a curse and will hurry off to a safer lake . . . allowing you to return alone and reel in all the fish you can tote home.

The Old School Chum Ploy

You're guaranteed to turn your rival anglers green with envy if you show up at a pristine fishing spot with a "chum." Chum is ground-up fish food frequently used to attract fish in saltwater. But what many fishermen don't know is that ground-up fish food made especially for certain varieties of freshwater fish is readily available. In fact, trout and catfish are raised in hatcheries on readily available "trout chow" and "catfish chow." When you show up at that bubbling trout stream with a 20-pound sack on your back clearly marked "trout chow," the other anglers will be checking their rule books. Not only will you drive them crazy with this sneaky trick, but the chum will really help you catch more fish.

It's Libel to Work

You say you've had enough of your neighbor's snide boasting and superior smile when he talks fishing? Then here's the perfect trick for you. Secretly slip an undersized fish on his stringer, and later call attention to it in front of others. If he's already publicly boasted about having caught "seven beauties," sneak a fish off his stringer and casually point out, "I guess you miscounted; I see only six."

If you're feeling particularly brazen, slip a partially thawed frozen fish on his stringer, and at a strategic moment say, "Gee, this fish seems awfully cold." Keep up the pressure and you'll wipe that superior smile off his face—and probably turn him to some sissy sport like badminton.

The Big Gulp

You're back at the dock and you've got one weenie-little fish. Meanwhile, your neighbor not only is bragging about the big one he caught, but has told you in tortuous detail what he did right and what you did wrong. Then he makes the wrong move. He leaves his fish in his cooler by the cleaning table and goes off to find someone else to bore with his bragging. You strike—quickly filleting his catch. When he returns, you act flustered and say, "Geez, I don't know how I got confused. But our coolers look alike and I just reached in and started cutting." When he gets done howling (the first time), graciously offer to take a photo of him holding up the skeleton. He'll howl some more.

Night Moves

The evening before a tourney, move a critical marker that steers boaters away from a reef or shallow bar. Don't take it away completely; just shift it a few strategic feet, then stick it back in. The next morning you'll chortle as your rivals roar up to the marker— only to run aground and tear up their engines.

The Big Bang

Although some fishermen have been known to drop sticks of dynamite overboard, that dirty trick could backfire. Almost as effective, and far safer, is to strategically lob a powerful M-80 firecracker into the water. The key is to quickly grab the stunned fish as they float to the surface—then look very innocent when fellow anglers run up asking, "What the hell was that?" It's best to simply say, "Got me, I haven't a clue," as opposed to "Must have been those beans I had for lunch."

Gas–Tastrophes

There are many ways to wreck your opponents' gasoline supply, ensuring victory as they get stranded somewhere on the water. You can always resort to the old sugar-in-the-gas-tank trick, but an easier method is to merely dislodge the gas line from an opponent's engine the night before. Sure, he'll find it, but not before he starts tearing his hair out wondering why his engine won't catch. Meanwhile, you're already out on the water, reelin' 'em in.

The Handyman Special

A must in every cheater's tackle box is a special homemade "lure" for those days when you can see the fish—but they won't bite. Crudely fashion a small piece of plastic into something barely resembling a fish, then hang two huge treble hooks on the back. This is nothing more than an illegal set of "snatch hooks" used to snag fish—but your feeble attempt at making it a lure beats the law. To really enjoy this sneaky trick, make sure you hold up your contraption so your fellow fishermen can see it. And when you start raking in fish, gush loudly: "Wow, what a great lure this is." They'll be driven into a frenzy because they know what you're doing—and can't do anything about it.

A Wee–Wee Problem

Wait for your rival's call of nature. As he moves to the edge of the boat to answer the call, you suddenly move to the opposite side and begin rocking the boat. It's a guaranteed accident and your obviously insincere "Sorry," accompanied by a guffaw, will only make him more P.O.'d. OK, maybe it won't wreck his fishing, but it'll sure wreck his peace of mind . . .

Play Balls

Slashing the tires or smashing the lights on a foe's trailer could get you in trouble with the law, but there are safer ways to disable it and keep him off the water. Simply change the steel ball on his trailer hitch—it'll drive him batty! If he has a 2-inch ball, stealthily replace it with a 1 7/8-inch ball. He won't notice the tiny difference in diameter when he hooks his boat up to his car—but it'll bounce off the ball at the first road bump and rip loose his taillight wires! If he has the

smaller ball, change it to the larger one. You'll hear his exasperated cursing for miles as he struggles to hitch up his boat.

The Bait and Switch

Buy a bait bucket that's EXACTLY identical to your opponent's. If the day's fishing calls for fat shiners, fill your bucket with skinny minnows. If everyone plans to use little minnows, put in nightcrawlers. Your foe, of course, will fill his bucket with the right bait for the occasion . . . but he won't get to keep it! After you arrive at the fishing spot, wait until he's distracted launching his boat and switch your dead-ringer bucket for his. When he gets out on the water and sees he's brought the wrong bait, his angry red face will light up the lake! The confused guy might even rush to a doctor with the fear that he's getting Alzheimer's.

Line Dance

A crude, but effective dirty trick, popular with Three Stooges fans, involves snagging a boat's mooring lines. There are several variations of this trick, but all involve your foe zipping away—only to get whiplash when he snaps to a halt because you've tied his boat line to a tree, dock, or piling. You can pull this off even in his driveway! If he's the fussy type who gets everything ready on his boat and trailer the night before, then comes out in the predawn hours and jumps in his car, he's yours. Just run a rope from his back trailer axle to the nearest tree, boulder, or other immovable object. With luck, he may even break the trailer axle, wreck the boat, and throw out his car's rear end. You can also pull this off when his boat's in the water— just loop a line (which you've brought) on the eyelet that most boats have on the back of the transom. He'll never notice it—until he starts away from the dock and almost takes the dock with him because you've tied that line to a piling. A guaranteed crowd pleaser.

Snakes Alive

You'd have to be lower than a snake's belly to drop a serpent in a nice-guy fisherman's livewell—but on the other hand, an obnoxious loudmouth deserves it. Simply buy or catch a blacksnake (or some other large-but-harmless reptile) and quietly deposit it in the creep's livewell. When he eyeballs the slippery critter, you'll hear his yell all the way back on shore—and his nerves will be shot the rest of the day.

Lured Away

Put a crimp in your foe's fishing style by asking to see his special hook or lure. Unknown to him, you've palmed a pair of mini-pliers—and as you "admire" his lure, you quickly clamp down and flatten the hook barbs. Your opponent will lose fish after fish before he closely examines his lure and spots the problem. Naturally he'll suspect sabotage, but you look baffled and say: "Wow, what the heck did you HOOK ONTO?"

Fly Ball

O.K., so you've got an insufferable neighbor who views himself as Mr. Trout—an authority on flies, "reading" the water, and every other aspect of trout fishing. What to do about his pontificating? Challenge him to a fish-off! You know you can't beat him honestly, so here's what to do: Collect some live flies that aren't native to the stream you plan to fish in. As you reach the bank, wait until he's not looking and strew a handful of flies out onto the water. Then yell, "Hey, what are those things?" Your neighbor won't want to admit he doesn't have a clue what they are, and he'll go crazy trying to "match the hatch." While he's doing this, you wander upstream and reel in the big ones—using the flies.

Bee's Wax

Always keep a wary eye peeled for an active hornet's nest in a tree hanging over the water. When you locate one, it cries out to be put to good use—and good use is payback to any bigmouth who's bothered you on the water. It's easy: Just tell Mr. Fisherman how you saw the biggest bass (trout, etc.) you've ever seen "right under that tree over there. He's still there, way back in," you tell him, "but I just couldn't catch him no matter what I tried." Then you leave. Enough said. Within minutes he'll be trying to put a perfect cast under that tree. And he'll get closer and closer, hoping to see the huge fish. He's bound to disturb those hornets, and he'll soon be getting a fish-eye view of any finny denizens in that area—as he jumps overboard to avoid the hornet swarm he's stirred up.

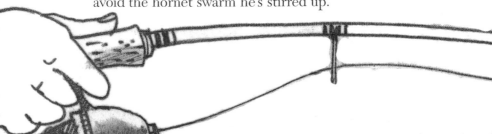

Prop Out

All right, you've had enough and you're not gonna take it anymore . . . but what to do? Here's a simple trick that will leave your foe stranded on the water, never suspecting what happened. Just pull the cotter pin on his engine. It's the pin that holds the prop on. Any marina can point out the cotter pin on his type of engine for you. Once you locate it, just approach it at night, yank it out, and leave. He'll roar off in the morning and everything will seem fine. But at some point, very quickly, that prop will fall off his engine and sink. He'll be stranded and will need a tow back in. You can be there to gloat, replying to his story of what happened with, "Gee, I always double-check my cotter pin and carry a spare."